D0597384

Questions and Answers: Countries

The Dominican Republic

A Question and Answer Book

by Kremena Spengler

Consultant:
Dr. Ramona Hernandez
Director, CUNY Dominican Studies Institute
and Associate Professor of Sociology
The City College of New York
New York, New York

Capstone press

Mankato, Minnesota

Fact Finders is published by Capstone Press,
151 Good Counsel Drive, P.O. Box 669, Mankato, Minnesota 56002.
www.capstonepress.com

Library of Congress Cataloging-in-Publication Data
Spengler, Kremena.
    The Dominican Republic : a question and answer book / by Kremena Spengler.
    p. cm.—(Fact finders. Questions and answers. Countries)
    Summary: "Describes the geography, history, economy, and culture of the
    Dominican Republic in a question-and-answer format"–Provided by publisher.
    Includes bibliographical references and index.
    ISBN-13: 978-0-7368-4353-9 (hardcover)
    ISBN-10: 0–7368–4353–1 (hardcover)
    1. Dominican Republic—Juvenile literature. I. Title. II. Series.
F1934.2.S64 2006
972.93—dc22   2005001164

Editorial Credits
Silver Editions, editorial, design, and production; Kia Adams, set designer; Ortelius Design,
Inc., cartographer; Wanda Winch, photo researcher; Scott Thoms, photo editor

Photo Credits
Art Directors/Ask Images, 23; Helene Rogers, 1, 4, 6, 25
Beryl Goldberg, 15, 17, 27
Corbis/Catherine Karnow, 11, 13; Ludovic Maisant, 7; Tom Bean, 18–19
Getty Images Inc./AFP/Vanderlei Almeida, 9
Houserstock/Hank Barone, 21; Steve Bly, cover (background)
Index Stock Imagery/Timothy O'Keefe, cover (foreground)
One Mile Up, Inc., 29 (flag)
Photo Courtesy of Paul Baker, 29 (coins)
Photo Courtesy of Richard Sutherland, 29 (bill)

Artistic Effects:
Photodisc/Jules Frazier, 18; PhotoLink, 16

1 2 3 4 5 6 10 09 08 07 06 05

Table of Contents

Features

Where is the Dominican Republic?

The Dominican Republic is on the island of Hispaniola in the Caribbean Sea. The country is about twice as large as the state of New Hampshire.

The Dominican Republic has many landforms. It has chains of forested mountains. Crops grow on the flat valleys and plains. Sandy beaches line the coast.

The Dominican Republic has hundreds of beaches.

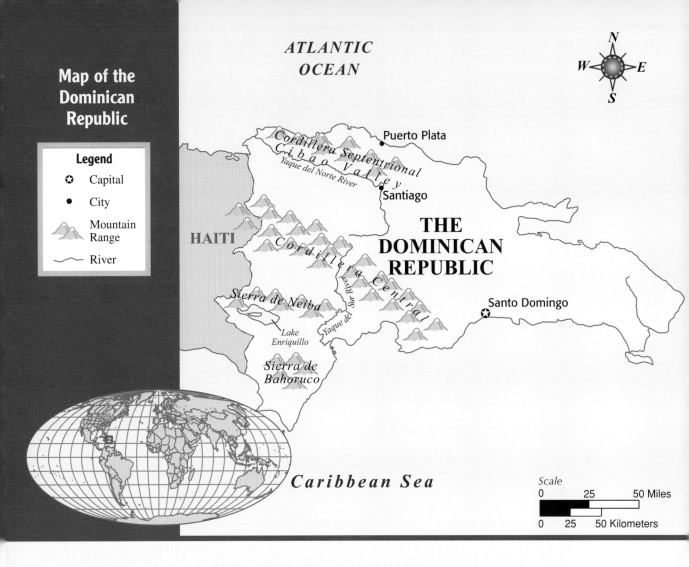

Map of the Dominican Republic

Legend
- ✪ Capital
- ● City
- 🏔 Mountain Range
- ～ River

ATLANTIC OCEAN

N
W · E
S

Cordillera Septentrional
Cibao Valley
Yaque del Norte River
Puerto Plata
Santiago

HAITI

THE DOMINICAN REPUBLIC

Cordillera Central

Sierra de Neiba
Yaque del Sur River
Lake Enriquillo

Sierra de Bahoruco

Santo Domingo

Caribbean Sea

Scale
0   25   50 Miles
0   25   50 Kilometers

The Dominican Republic has warm weather all year. Temperatures in the mountains are cooler than at the coast.

The country receives a great deal of rain. **Hurricanes** are violent storms that bring heavy rain and strong wind to the island.

When did the Dominican Republic become a country?

The Dominican Republic became a country in 1844. Before then, it was ruled at different times by Spain and Haiti.

Christopher Columbus landed on the island in 1492. He called it Hispaniola and made it a Spanish **colony**. The western end of Hispaniola became Haiti in 1804.

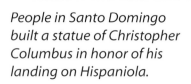

People in Santo Domingo built a statue of Christopher Columbus in honor of his landing on Hispaniola.

Juan Pablo Duarte is known as the founder of the Dominican Republic. A statue of Duarte is in Santo Domingo.

In 1822, the Haitians took over the whole island. In 1844, forces controlled by Juan Pablo Duarte drove the Haitians out. Duarte formed the Dominican Republic.

The colony joined Spain again in 1861. Many Dominicans fought Spanish rule. In 1865, Spain gave up the colony.

What type of government do Dominicans have?

The Dominican Republic's government is a **democracy**. Once every four years, the people choose a president and vice president. The president carries out the country's laws. The president names a **cabinet**. Cabinet members run parts of the government.

Fact!

Dominicans must vote if they are 18 or older or if they are married. Police and people in the armed forces cannot vote.

Former President Leonel Fernandez gives a speech before the National Congress.

The National Congress makes the country's laws. It has two groups. Dominicans vote for the 32 members of the Senate. They also vote for the 150 members of the House of Deputies. Both groups serve for four years.

What kind of housing do Dominicans have?

Most city people live in houses or apartments. These homes usually have electricity and running water.

People from rural places move to cities to look for work. Some build homes from cardboard. The government is trying to build them better homes.

Where do people in the Dominican Republic live?

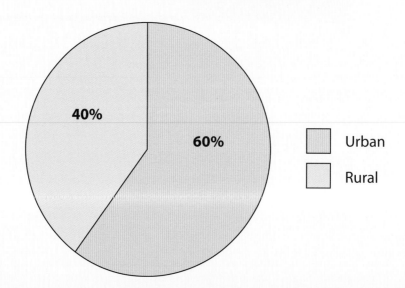

40%

60%

Urban

Rural

Colorfully painted houses can be found in rural areas.

In rural areas, most people live in small farmhouses. Some homes have floors made of dirt. Many homes are painted in bright colors. Few have electricity or running water.

What are Dominican forms of transportation?

Dominicans travel by bus, van, or truck. Smaller buses, called *gua–guas*, are a good and cheap way to travel from town to town. Motorcycles are also common. People can even hire a motorcycle taxi.

Owning a car is not common in the Dominican Republic. Few people have money to pay for one. Car travel is not easy. Only about half of the roads are paved.

Fact!

Trains ship crops, such as sugarcane, from the fields to the mills.

Motorcycle taxi is an easy way to travel short distances.

Airports and seaports serve **tourists**. Large jets land at airports in Santo Domingo and Puerto Plata. These cities' seaports also welcome visitors traveling by ship.

What are the Dominican Republic's industries?

Tourism is the Dominican Republic's main industry. The country's beaches and mountains bring visitors to the island. Dominicans earn more money from tourism than from any other industry.

The Dominican Republic has deposits of gold, silver, and nickel. These **natural resources** help its mining industry.

What does the Dominican Republic import and export?	
Imports	*Exports*
chemicals	cacao
cotton and cloth	coffee
food	gold
oil	sugar

A waitress serves tourists in a Santo Domingo restaurant.

Farming is another large industry in the Dominican Republic. Farmers grow coffee, rice, tobacco, and many fruits.

One of the country's main crops is sugarcane. Mills turn sugarcane into sugar. Sugar is then **exported** to other countries.

What is school like in the Dominican Republic?

Dominican children must go to elementary school for six years. They start school at age 7. After elementary school, some students go on to six years of high school.

Students may choose from several kinds of high schools. Most high schools prepare students for college. Others prepare them to become teachers or other kinds of workers.

Fact!

Poor children in rural areas may not be able to finish elementary school. Many schools in rural areas do not have all six grades. Other children may have to leave school to go to work.

These students attend a small private school in Santo Domingo.

The Dominican Republic has public and private schools. Public schools are free, but high school students must buy their own books. Private schools charge money. The Catholic church runs most private schools. Private schools have better teachers, buildings, and books.

What are the Dominicans' favorite sports and games?

Baseball is the Dominican Republic's favorite sport. Most towns have baseball fields where people of all ages play.

Sammy Sosa, Pedro Martinez, and other U.S. baseball stars were born in the Dominican Republic. Many Dominican boys want to be like them. They see baseball as a way to a better life.

Fact!

In 2004, Sammy Sosa was placed seventh on the all-time home run list. He had 574 home runs.

Dominicans of all ages enjoy playing baseball.

Dominicans also like basketball. The professional season runs from June to August. Yet, many people play all year.

The country's mountains and beaches are good places for outdoor activities. Dominicans enjoy hikes and walks. They fish, swim, and surf along the coast.

What are traditional Dominican art forms?

Music and dance are the best-known art forms in the Dominican Republic. Merengue is fast and happy dance music. Merengue bands have a drum, a metal **guiro**, and other instruments. *Bachata* is a slower kind of Dominican dance music.

Fact!

Juan Luis Guerra is a world-famous Dominican musician. Guerra won three Grammys at the 2000 Latin Grammy Awards.

A merengue band plays at an outdoor theater.

Many writers come from the Dominican Republic. Manuel de Jesus Galvan wrote *Enriquillo.* The book is about an island hero. Don Pedro Mir wrote poems about different periods in the history of the Dominican Republic. Joaquin Balaguer and Juan Bosch were both writers and presidents.

What major holidays do Dominicans celebrate?

Dominicans celebrate freedom from Haiti on Independence Day, February 27. They celebrate freedom from Spain on Restoration Day, August 16. People hold parades on both holidays.

What other holidays do people in the Dominican Republic celebrate?

Columbus Day
Duarte Day
New Year's Day
Our Lady of Altagracia
Pan-American Day
United Nations Day

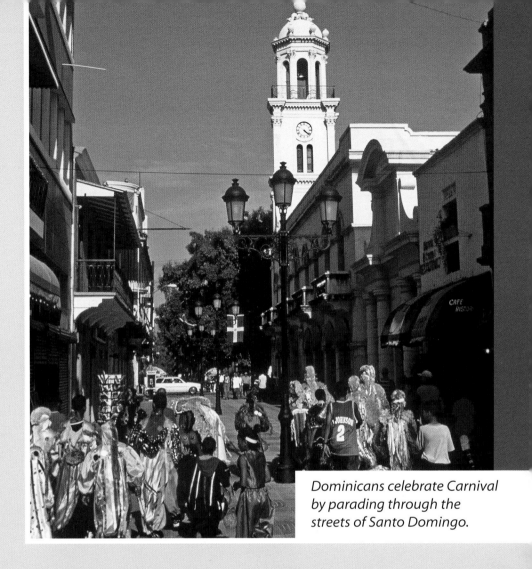

Dominicans celebrate Carnival by parading through the streets of Santo Domingo.

Most Dominicans are Catholic. They celebrate Christian holidays. Many go to church on Christmas and Easter. Dominicans enjoy Carnival before Lent. They dance in the streets. They parade in costumes and ride on floats.

What are traditional Dominican foods?

The best-known Dominican meal is *la bandera*, "the flag." This dish has red beans, white rice, meat, and green **plantains**. The four parts of the meal are like the four parts of the country's flag.

Fact!

Plantains look like bananas, but they are not as sweet. They must be cooked before they are eaten.

Dominican families often prepare meals together.

Goat meat is very popular. It is roasted or stewed with spices. For special occasions, Dominicans prepare *sanchocho*. This soup has vegetables and seven kinds of meat.

Dominicans enjoy fruits such as mango and pineapple. They boil them in sweetened water as a dessert.

What is family life like in the Dominican Republic?

Dominican families are very close. Often two or three **generations** of a family live in the same house. Usually, the oldest man is head of the family.

In some families, women stay home to care for the family. The men work outside the home.

What are the ethnic backgrounds of people in the Dominican Republic?

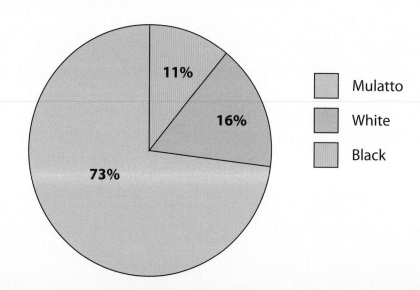

11%

16%

73%

Mulatto

White

Black

Dominican families enjoy getting together for picnics in a park.

Dominican children form strong family ties based on **baptism**. A child's godparents are like a second set of parents. They form lasting ties with the child. Godparents often help with the child's schooling, money, and job.

Fast Facts

Official name:

The Dominican Republic

Land area:

18,680 square miles
(48,380 square kilometers)

Average annual precipitation (Santo Domingo):

55.1 inches (140 centimeters)

Average January temperature (Santo Domingo):

75 degrees Fahrenheit
(24 degrees Celsius)

Average July temperature (Santo Domingo):

81 degrees Fahrenheit
(27 degrees Celsius)

Population:

8,833,634 people

Capital city:

Santo Domingo

Language:

Spanish

Natural resources:

gold, nickel, silver

Religions:

Roman Catholic	95%
Other	5%

Money and Flag

Money:

The Dominican Republic's money is the Dominican peso. In 2005, 1 U.S. dollar equaled about 28 Dominican pesos. One Canadian dollar equaled about 23 Dominican pesos.

Flag:

The Dominican flag has four rectangles divided by a white cross. The blue rectangles stand for freedom. The red rectangles stands for the blood shed for the country's freedom. The Dominican coat of arms is at the center of the cross.

Learn to Speak Spanish

People in the Dominican Republic speak Spanish. Learn to speak some Spanish words using the chart below.

English	Spanish	Pronunciation
good morning	buenos días	(BWAY-nohs DEE-ahs)
good-bye	adiós	(ah-dee-OHS)
please	por favor	(POR fah-VOR)
thank you	gracias	(GRAH-see-us)
How are you?	¿Cómo estás?	(KOH-moh ay-STAHS)
I'm fine	Bien	(BEE-en)

Glossary

baptism (BAP-tiz-uhm)—a religious ceremony for admitting a person into a Christian church

cabinet (KAB-in-it)—a group of advisers for the head of government

colony (KOL-uh-nee)—an area that is settled by people from another country and that is ruled by that country

democracy (di-MOK-ruh-see)—a form of government in which people choose their leaders

export (EK-sport)—to send and sell goods to other countries

generation (jen-uh-RAY-shun)—a group of persons born around the same time

guiro (GWEE-roh)—an instrument traditionally made from a gourd and played by scraping a stick along its surface; today, some guiros are made of metal.

hurricane (HUR-uh-kane)—a severe wind and rainstorm that starts on the ocean

natural resource (NACH-ur-uhl REE-sorss)—a material found in nature that is useful to people

plantain (PLAN-tuhn)—a tropical fruit that looks like a banana but is eaten cooked

tourist (TOOR-ist)—a person who is traveling for pleasure or to learn about places

Internet Sites

FactHound offers a safe, fun way to find Internet sites related to this book. All of the sites on FactHound have been researched by our staff.

Here's how:
1. Visit *www.facthound.com*
2. Type in this special code **0736843531** for age-appropriate sites. Or enter a search word related to this book for a more general search.
3. Click on the **Fetch It** button.

FactHound will fetch the best sites for you!

Read More

De Capua, Sarah. *The Dominican Republic.* Discovering Cultures. New York: Benchmark Books, 2004.

Englar, Mary. *The Dominican Republic.* Many Cultures, One World. Mankato, Minn.: Blue Earth Books, 2004.

McCarthy, Pat. *The Dominican Republic.* Top Ten Countries of Recent Immigrants. Berkeley Heights, N.J.: MyReportLinks.com Books, 2004.

Savage, Jeff. *Sammy Sosa.* Amazing Athletes. Minneapolis: LernerSports, 2005.

Index